LOVING
Your Husband

*Building
an Intimate
Marriage
in a Fallen
World*

A Bible Study for Women by
Cynthia Heald

NAVPRESS ●
BRINGING TRUTH TO LIFE
NavPress Publishing Group
P.O.Box35001, Colorado Springs, Colorado 80935

The Navigators is an international Christian organization. Our mission is to reach, disciple, and equip people to know Christ and to make Him known through successive generations. We envision multitudes of diverse people in the United States and every other nation who have a passionate love for Christ, live a lifestyle of sharing Christ's love, and multiply spiritual laborers among those without Christ.

NavPress is the publishing ministry of The Navigators. NavPress publications help believers learn biblical truth and apply what they learn to their lives and ministries. Our mission is to stimulate spiritual formation among our readers.

(Originally published as *Eve, Out of Eden.*)

Scripture quotations in this publication are from the *New American Standard Bible* (NASB), © The Lockman Foundation 1960, 1962, 1963, 1968, 1971, 1972, 1973, 1975, 1977. Other versions used are: *The Amplified Bible* (AMP), © The Lockman Foundation 1954, 1958; the *Holy Bible: New International Version* (NIV), copyright © 1973, 1978, 1984, International Bible Society, used by permission of Zondervan Bible Publishers; and the *Revised Standard Version Bible* (RSV), copyright 1946, 1952, 1971, by the Division of Christian Education of the National Council of the Churches of Christ in the USA, used by permission, all rights reserved.

Printed in the United States of America

14 15 16 17 18 19 20 / 00 99 98 97

CONTENTS

AUTHOR

Cynthia Hall Heald is a native Texan. She and her husband, Jack, a veterinarian by profession, are on full-time staff with The Navigators in Tucson, Arizona. They have four children: Melinda, Daryl, Shelly, and Michael.

Cynthia graduated from the University of Texas with a B.A. in English. She speaks frequently to church women's groups and at seminars and retreats.

Cynthia is also the author of the popular Bible studies *Becoming a Woman of Excellence, Becoming a Woman of Freedom, Becoming a Woman of Purpose,* and *Intimacy with God,* and co-author of *Loving Your Wife.* She has also authored a devotional entitled *Abiding in Christ.*

PREFACE

Eve's marriage began in a beautiful garden, yet she and Adam lived most of it in stark reality outside of this garden called Eden.

As Eve's daughters who have chosen marriage, we too must live out of Eden—the idyllic garden has been exchanged for a world full of challenges and temptations. How are we to see ourselves against the contemporary profile of a wife in today's world? Are the Scriptures relevant to existing lifestyles and needs?

I have written this study to focus on biblical insights concerning the role, purpose, and influence of a Christian wife. My prayer is that you will be encouraged to consider God's Word in a fresh way and to seek to honor the Lord and your husband in freedom and love.

This study has impacted my life and my relationship to my husband, Jack, in a very special way. I have discovered that a wife rightly related to her Lord will be a wife rightly related to her husband.

May your life and marriage be enriched in studying *Loving Your Husband*.

SUGGESTIONS FOR HOW TO USE THIS STUDY

The purpose of *Loving Your Husband* is to help you understand how to become a godly wife in today's world. Through exploring key Scripture passages, reflecting on your personal situation, and considering the insights of godly writers, you will have opportunity to discover biblical truth and apply it in the joys as well as the struggles of your life as a married woman.

You'll come across the following sections in each lesson:

Insight into Scripture. This part of your study will take you to key scriptures relevant to the topic at hand. Keep in mind that reference aids—such as a study Bible, a general commentary, a Bible dictionary—can greatly assist you in understanding and interpreting God's Word. You will also need access to a standard dictionary to help you define key words and concepts.

Insight into myself. Here you will be asked to reflect on your attitudes and circumstances in order to examine areas of your life addressed by a given lesson.

Be honest and thoughtful; the purpose of this section is simply to help you understand yourself. You may want to keep some of these answers between yourself and the Lord, or share them with one close friend. Answer them based on the way you are, not on the way you think you

9

should be. Remember that becoming a godly wife is a *lifelong process* through God's work in you.

As you approach these questions, pray for God's wisdom in revealing to you those aspects of your behavior or perspectives in which He desires you to be especially open to the work of His Holy Spirit.

Insight into my husband. This group of questions will deepen your awareness of how you and your spouse relate to each other by asking you to reflect on issues from your husband's point of view.

Your answers here will complement the insights you uncover about yourself, and they may also reveal areas in which you need to know more about how your husband thinks or what he feels. If you don't know and can't guess at an answer, consider asking your husband for his response, if you feel the freedom to do so. This could open up some healthy communication and provide you both with a "good excuse" for talking over some things you might otherwise not have gotten around to discussing.

Insight from an older woman. In this section you'll find a personal reflection from me, often with an anecdote to help you learn from my life experiences. This part of the study, which contains challenges, encouragements, explanations, cautions—even confessions!—gives you the chance to follow the friendly voice of a woman who has been across this territory already and can help point the way.

Included throughout this study are excerpts from godly and insightful writers on the marriage relationship. Use them to stimulate your thinking, reinforce what you're learning, and enhance your understanding in those areas that seem particularly troublesome or uncertain to you.

This study has been designed for you to use individually or in a group. The companion study for husbands, *Loving Your Wife* (available from NavPress), is also designed for individual or group use. The two studies have enough common material and focus to be used together, and are flexible enough to be used in several different ways. Here are some ideas:

1. Use *Loving Your Husband* on your own, perhaps

choosing a trusted woman friend with whom to share your responses.

2. Go through *Loving Your Husband* in a small group composed of married women. Rotate leadership and place the emphasis on sharing experiences, insights, reactions, questions, etc., as you provide encouragement, challenge, accountability, and prayer support for each other.

3. Work through *Loving Your Husband* while your husband works through *Loving Your Wife*. Share your responses with each other and discuss what you're learning and how you're reacting to the insights offered by the author and the writers quoted. Since the chapters in each study work together but can also stand alone, you and your husband could select only those chapters you feel would be most beneficial if you decide not to go through the whole study all in one period of time.

4. Go through these two studies in a mixed small group of couples. This arrangement could be very stimulating, but because of the many variables involved (wives and husbands, two different studies) you would need to plan carefully and structure your time for maximum benefit. The group would most likely function more effectively if members knew each other and had established at least some level of rapport before your sessions started. Leadership of the group could be assigned to either couples or individuals.

You might consider having each couple go over their lessons with each other at home before meeting with the group. Or, when you convene, first break up the group into two smaller groups of all wives and of all husbands. Then get everyone together for a summary from each contingent regarding major questions and insights, followed by general group discussion.

Of course, you could simply open up the group each time with an open-ended, free-for-all discussion of what-ever members wanted to go over, but you would need an especially competent group leader well-versed in the art of controlling, stimulating, and moderating group discussion and interaction. With both wives and husbands present, and two different studies from which to draw, you would probably not run out of things to talk about in an average session.

Sprinkling an occasional purely-social outing into a group like this could enliven your fellowship with each other, create a more comfortable environment for regular sessions, and provide husbands and wives with an outlet for spending some recreational time together in a group context.

No matter how you use this study, above all pray for God's guidance and grace in using it to make you a wife more fully devoted to glorifying Him.

"Whom Have I in Heaven But You?"

Whom have I in Heaven but You? And I have no delight or desire on earth beside You. My flesh and my heart may fail, but God is the rock and firm strength of my heart, and my portion for ever.

Psalm 73:25-26 (AMP)

And all we need to live as Christians, no matter what our circumstances, is the security of His love and the significance of participation in His purpose. We must never claim that our relationships with others do not affect us deeply: they do. But Christ's resources are enough to keep us going.[1]

Lawrence J. Crabb, Jr.

"No one told me that after marriage came life!"
"After moonlight and roses, come daylight and dishes." These are great commentaries on the reality of marriage. Larry Crabb states that many of us stand at the altar and silently repeat the vow, "I give myself to you for the rest of my life for you to meet all of my needs." We all have profound, demanding needs that cry to be satisfied. Naively, we think that if we marry, all our needs will be met. I remember the first time Jack, my husband, and I had a disagreement after our wedding. He smiled and commented, "Well, the honeymoon is over!" All too soon, we realize that the "honeymoon" cannot last forever and that we are still individuals with specific needs. If these needs cannot be fully satisfied in marriage, then where do we go with our feelings of wanting to be loved and to be accepted as someone of value?

Insight into Scripture

1. When Jesus met the woman at the well, He saw a woman in great need. Her spirit was thirsting, yet with all her striving she was not satisfied. Read John 4:7-30. Write a brief description of the Samaritan woman's life before she encountered Jesus—what need was she trying to meet, and how was she seeking fulfillment in her life?

2. What was Jesus' response to this woman's need?

3. To find out more about the Samaritan woman, read farther into the chapter—4:39-42. How do you think her life changed after her encounter with the Lord?

4. As the Lord becomes our source of refreshment and nourishment for our spirits, we become secure in who we are in Christ. After studying the following verses, write down the thoughts conveyed in these scriptures concerning God's sufficiency in our lives.

Psalm 27:1

Psalm 56

Psalm 62:1-2

Colossians 2:9-10

Colossians 3:1-3

5. When we are depending upon the Lord to meet our deepest needs, Paul's words found in Philippians 2:3-4 and 4:4-7 take on new meaning. Study these passages and write a paragraph summarizing your thoughts on how these verses speak to you as a woman in Christ who is married.

> It is a foolish woman who expects her husband to be
> to her that which only Jesus Christ Himself can be:
> always ready to forgive, totally understanding, unend-
> ingly patient, invariably tender and loving, unfailing
> in every area, anticipating every need, and making
> more than adequate provision. Such expectations put
> a man under an impossible strain.[2]
> Ruth Bell Graham

Insight into myself

6. It is important that we examine ourselves and understand how we respond to our husbands. Throughout
this study as you come to this section in each lesson,
ponder and pray over these questions designed to
reveal your attitudes and your particular circumstances.

a. How would I describe my deepest needs and
longings?

b. How do I tend to satisfy my needs? On whom do I
depend?

c. How do I think God views my dependence on Him?

d. When I feel that my husband has failed to meet my needs, how do I react? What do I do when he fails me?

e. How can I begin to experience more of God's sufficiency in my life?

For one of the most profound ways in which the Lord touches us and teaches us about Himself and His own essential otherness is through the very limits He has placed upon our relationships with one another. It is an enormous source of human frustration that our need for intimacy far outstrips its capacity to be met in other people. Primarily what keeps us separate is our sin, but there is also another factor, and that is that in each one of us the holiest and neediest and most sensitive place of all has been made and is reserved for God alone, so that only He can enter there. No one else can love us as He does, and no one can be the sort of Friend to us that He is.[3]
Mike Mason

Insight into my husband

7. In order to gain greater insight into your marriage, carefully consider these questions concerning your husband's attitudes and perspectives. This section occurs in each lesson and will complement the insights you discover about yourself. If you're not sure how your husband would answer, and if you feel free to do so, you might ask him what his answer would be.

a. What are my husband's deepest needs and longings?

b. In what ways do I minister to his needs?

c. Does my husband feel that he measures up to my expectations of a "good husband"? Why or why not?

d. What is one change I can make to deepen my sensitivity and ministry to my husband?

> Husbands and wives are to regard marriage as an opportunity to minister in a unique and special way to another human being, to be used of God to bring their spouses into a more satisfying appreciation of their worth as persons who are secure and significant in Jesus Christ.[4]
>
> Lawrence J. Crabb, Jr.

Insight from an older woman

I waited impatiently in the coffee shop. My husband, Jack, was very late. After a futile phone call home, I realized that he had probably forgotten to pick me up. I asked the young woman with whom I was meeting if she would mind taking me to the church.

When I arrived, I slipped into the pew by Jack, and he smiled and patted my shoulder. I could tell that it still had not dawned on him that he had forgotten me!

I share this example from my life because it graphically portrays the truth that no one, not even a godly husband, can be counted on to be perfect. At that time, however, I felt unloved and abandoned. If Jack *really* loved me, how could he have forgotten me?

It is vital that we understand that our husbands cannot fully satisfy our needs. Our husbands can minister to us in special ways; they can provide feelings of love and acceptance; but the fact of our worth can only be founded on the unconditional love that God alone can give. As I abide in the Lord's unshakable, secure love, then I can love and serve Jack without the expectation that he must love and serve me back in the same way. None of us is perfect, so we must go to the Perfect One to be fulfilled.

We ought to be comfortable to live with, because we are not demanding, but understanding. Controlled by Jesus Christ, we are free from obsession with self, and can listen, love, and pray.

Our basic fulfillment does not come from marriage, from prestige, from position, or from possessions. It comes as we are so indwelt by God that his fellowship meets our inner need and we experience the outworking of his love through us.[5]

Gladys M. Hunt

NOTES
1. Lawrence J. Crabb, Jr., *The Marriage Builder* (Grand Rapids: Zondervan Publishing House, 1982), page 36.
2. Ruth Bell Graham, *It's My Turn* (Old Tappan, N.J.: Fleming H. Revell Company, 1982), page 74.
3. Mike Mason, *The Mystery of Marriage* (Portland, Oreg.: Multnomah Press, 1985), page 33.
4. Crabb, *Marriage Builder,* page 52.
5. Gladys M. Hunt, "She Has No Equal," in *The Marriage Affair,* J. Allan Petersen ed. (Wheaton, Ill.: Tyndale House Publishers, 1971), page 96.

"The Wise Woman Builds Her House"

*The wise woman builds her house,
But the foolish tears it down with
her own hands.*

Proverbs 14:1

*Until I am aware that my needs
are already met in Christ, I will be
motivated by emptiness to meet my
needs. When by simple faith I
accept Christ's shed blood as full
payment for my sins, I am brought
into a relationship with an infinite
Being of love and purpose who
fully satisfies my deepest needs for
security and significance.
Therefore I am freed from self-
centered preoccupation with my
own needs; they are met. It is now
possible for me to give to others out
of my fullness rather than needing
to receive from others because of
my emptiness. For the first time, I
have the option of living selflessly.*[1]

Lawrence J. Crabb, Jr.

A woman who understands what is true, right, and lasting creates and establishes a home for her husband and family where security, encouragement, and peace dwell. I believe that God has equipped us, as wives, to build in such a way that our lives will truly take on eternal significance because we choose to honor Him by building wisely. It is interesting to me that the excellent wife described in Proverbs 31 is praised by her husband and children—evidence that her primary ministry was to build her home in wisdom. To do this takes personal discipline, perseverance, and acceptance of "the option of living selflessly." But it is in giving that we are blessed, and it is in being the woman God created us to be that we are fulfilled.

Insight into Scripture

1. A wise woman who builds her home must consider her own preparation as a builder.

   a. What key thoughts are communicated in the following verses about some necessary spiritual commitments in order to build wisely?

   Luke 6:46-49

   Luke 14:25-30

   2 Corinthians 5:14-15

   2 Timothy 2:15

b. How would each of these commitments help you in being a godly woman who builds wisely?

2. Proverbs 2:6 states, "For the LORD gives wisdom; from His mouth come knowledge and understanding."

   a. Read Psalm 119:97-105 and write down the psalmist's various responses to God's Word.

   b. How does this passage encourage you to strengthen your walk with the Lord and to grow in wisdom?

3. a. Proverbs 24:3-4 provides a verbal picture of building a house. Study these verses carefully (you might consult a dictionary and/or a commentary) and write down your thoughts about how wisdom, understanding, and knowledge contribute to building a house.

b. Refer to Proverbs 14:1. If a wise woman builds a house with wisdom, understanding, and knowledge, how does a foolish woman tear it down "with her own hands"?

---

4. The excellent wife portrayed in Proverbs 31 is praised because she feared the Lord. Proverbs 1:7 reminds us that "the fear of the LORD is the beginning of knowledge." This proper reverence and respect for the living God can be an essential motivating factor in our becoming wise builders.

a. What insights about how we build can be found in 1 Corinthians 3:10-15?

b. In what ways does this passage speak to you about the importance of how we build with our lives? (You might want to define gold, silver, and precious stones, and wood, hay, and stubble.)

It is one thing to feel chained to the dishpan, and another to feel that we have an important part in making a house a home. We can't hoax ourselves into feeling jolly about dishwater, but when a morning comes that we find ourselves singing over the sink and stacking the dishes with genuine indifference— or even with a kind of tenderness—then we know that we have stumbled upon the meaning of small tasks in the heavenly economy.[2]

Marguerite Harmon Bro

5. a. How do I view the cost involved in being a wise woman?

   b. Practically speaking, what do I do daily to gain wisdom?

   c. What are some specific ways I build in gold, silver, and precious stones?

   d. What is there in my life that produces wood, hay, and stubble? What can I do to begin to minimize this part of my life?

   e. If it is your goal to be a wise woman who builds, write out a prayer of commitment to the Lord expressing your feelings and desires.

There is no substitute for a life given over to Jesus Christ, for genuine relationship with God. A Christian woman is one who has gotten off the throne of her own life and let Jesus Christ reign there. There must be an interchange between the Lord and ourselves, a time of daily fellowship together. Meeting God each morning for a time of fellowship in the Bible and in prayer is vital to our Christian lives. We are not collecting facts, but becoming acquainted with our Lord. We are learning to understand righteous principles so that they can be worked out in our lives by the power of the Holy Spirit.[3]

Gladys M. Hunt

Insight into my husband

6. a. Is my husband able to discern my growth in Christ-likeness? Why or why not?

   b. In what ways is he aware of my desire to build him up so that he is encouraged and affirmed?

   c. How would my husband describe the way I "build" our home? Why?

d. What, if anything, is something I know he would like me to do differently in relation to him or to our home?

The Lord alone can give you these skills and abilities. You can't do it on your own. Working independently of Him will accomplish zero. Frustration and futility will haunt you if you try to do it in your own strength. Remember, it is the *Lord* who gives these gifts. Unless the *Lord* pulls it off, you labor in vain.[4]
Charles R. Swindoll

Insight from an older woman

If I am to be wise, I must allow Christ and His Word to give me the wisdom from above. I must take responsibility for the depth of my life with the Lord. Only as I grow and mature in Christ will I be equipped and prepared to build in gold and silver. I must focus more on being than on doing—for out of my heart flow the springs of life.

So I come to the Lord with the prayer that He would teach me, mold me, and lead me in being the wife my husband needs. I pray this because I have a very healthy fear of the Lord God. He has purchased my life with the blood of His Son, and I have willingly accepted His gift of love and have surrendered my life to Him because I love Him and know that He continually seeks my good. Just as I have never wanted to intentionally offend or dishonor my earthly father, so in a much deeper way I do not want to disgrace my heavenly Father by my life.

The key to being a faithful builder lies not in my own effort or striving, but in my choosing to be dependent upon the grace, wisdom, and strength I can receive from the Lord. I will one day give Him an account of how I lived my life, especially in my role as a wife. It is my desire to stand before God as a workman, a builder, a wife who will not need to be ashamed.

Unless the LORD builds the house, those who build it labor in vain. Unless the LORD watches over the city, the watchman stays awake in vain.
Psalm 127:1 (RSV)

NOTES
1. Lawrence J. Crabb, Jr., *The Marriage Builder* (Grand Rapids: Zondervan Publishing House, 1982), page 57.
2. Marguerite Harmon Bro, quoted in *The Marriage Affair,* J. Allan Petersen ed. (Wheaton, Ill.: Tyndale House Publishers, 1971), page 102.
3. Hunt, "She Has No Equal," in *The Marriage Affair,* Petersen ed., page 93.
4. Charles R. Swindoll, *Strike the Original Match* (Portland, Oreg.: Multnomah Press, 1980), page 25.

"I Will Make Him a Helper"

Then the LORD God said, "It is not good for the man to be alone; I will make him a helper suitable for him."

Genesis 2:18

That the woman was made of a rib out of the side of Adam; not made out of his head to rule over him, nor out of his feet to be trampled upon by him, but out of his side to be equal with him, under his arm to be protected, and near his heart to be beloved.[1]

Matthew Henry

LESSON 3 We as wives have been created by God to be helpers to our husbands. The Lord has specially formed us to complete our husbands by bringing them companionship in ways that no other human relationship can. It is important to study why women were originally created and to remind ourselves that wives are called to minister in unique ways to their husbands. "Helpmeet" has been defined as a companion who gives aid, who is cooperative, useful, and beneficial.

Insight into Scripture

1. After creating Adam, God placed him in the garden. Genesis 2:15-25 provides a detailed account of Eve's creation. Read this passage and use the questions below to help you think creatively about God's purposes in these events.

    a. Why do you think God gave the command found in verses 16-17 to Adam before He created Eve?

    b. Express your thoughts concerning why God said, "It is not good for the man to be alone" (verse 18).

    c. Define:

       helper—

       suitable—

    d. Describe how Adam might have felt when he realized that there was not a partner suitable for him (verse 20).

e. Why do you think God waited to create Eve?

f. What does "become one flesh" mean to you (verse 24)?

The Lord God made woman out of part of man's side and closed up the place with flesh, but in marriage He reopens this empty, aching place in man and begins the process of putting the woman back again, if not literally in the side, then certainly at it: permanently there, intrusively there, a sudden lifelong resident of a space which until that point the man will have considered to be his own private territory, even his own body. But in marriage he will cleave to the woman, and the woman to him, the way his own flesh cleaves to his own bones.

  Just so, says the Lord, do I Myself desire to invade your deepest privacy, binding you to Me all your life long and even into eternity with cords of blood.[2]
  Mike Mason

---

2. In order to be a helper suitable for our husbands, it is essential that we understand that we are not alone or helpless in the role that God has given us.

   a. What comfort or encouragement do the following verses offer us?

   Psalm 33:18-22

Isaiah 41:10

John 14:15-17

Romans 8:26-27

b. What conditions, if any, are mentioned in these verses if we are to receive help from the Lord?

---

3. A biblical job description of a Christian wife can be found in Titus 2:3-5. Write a brief paragraph telling how these seven things will be a help to husbands.

God adds that the one He would bring alongside Adam would be "suitable for him." Literally, "corresponding to" him. She would provide those missing pieces from the puzzle of his life. She would complete him as a qualified, corresponding partner. It is a beautiful picture of a dignified, necessary role filled by one whom God would make and bring alongside the man. In God's original design the plan was to have each partner distinct and unique, needing each other and therefore finding fulfillment with each other.[3]

Charles R. Swindoll

4. a. Am I content with God's creating me to be a helper to my husband? Why or why not?

   b. How do I appropriate God's strength in being a suitable helper for my husband?

   c. In light of Titus 2:3-5, in what ways do I help my husband?

   d. In what ways do I hinder my husband?

   e. Do I tend to be too helpful to my husband by nagging or mothering him? In what ways?

   f. How do I respond when my husband refuses my help?

   g. How am I individually suited to help my husband spiritually, emotionally, physically?

The natural resistance to truly giving ourselves to the other is rooted in our stubborn fear that if we really give, with no manipulative purpose, we will be short-changed. Our needs will not be met. At best we'll be disappointed; at worst, we'll be destroyed.

But God is faithful. We are to trust His perfect love to cast out our fear, believing that as we give to our spouse in His name, He will supernaturally bless us with an awareness of His presence. And He will. But it may take time—perhaps months—before we sense His work in us. The willingness to give uncon-ditionally does not come by simply deciding to be selfless. The stain of self-centeredness requires many washings before it no longer controls our motivation. Many commitments to minister and much time spent with God will transpire before we know what it means to *give*. Our job is to learn faithfulness and to press on in obedience, not giving in to discourage-ment or weariness, believing that God will always honor the conscious and persevering motivation to serve Him. When a spouse becomes critical, drinks more heavily, or rejects efforts of ministry, we are to continue in our obedience, believing that our responsibility before God is to obey and to trust Him for the outcome.[4]

Lawrence J. Crabb, Jr.

Insight into my husband

5. a. Does my husband view me as vitally interested in his life? Why or why not?

   b. What are some of the ways my husband would say I help or complete him?

c. Would my husband say that I tend to be *too* helpful? In what way?

d. In what areas would he like for me to better encourage or serve him?

e. Does my husband basically feel that I am *for* him? Why or why not?

> We women learn from the Bible that God created us to be a "help meet" for our husbands (Genesis 2:18). That is, a help suited to their needs. Since every man is different, needs will vary. So it is up to the wife to study her own husband to discover how she can best meet those needs.[5]
> Ruth Bell Graham

Insight from an older woman

"A man's house is his fortress in a warring world, where a woman's hand buckles on his armor in the morning and soothes his fatigue and wounds at night."[6] I read this observation by Frank Crane and thought that many wives would laugh at his words. Most husbands are fortunate to receive a warm greeting when they arrive home, much less any acknowledgment of their fatigue or wounds. (I speak from experience!)

With all the stress and pressures facing today's women, it's hard to think of helping anyone else—especially our husbands! I tend to view Jack as a healthy, mature adult who can take care of himself—and so I tend to forget that he needs me to be there for him. I find myself becoming complacent in taking the initiative to help and encourage him creatively. Because I have experienced the love of God in my life and I trust His plan, His goodness, and His provision for my needs, I desire to be a helper suitable to my husband and to stand guard at his fortress.

We are not alone when it comes to other people, and neither are we alone when it comes to God. However much we may wish at times to be left alone, it is not an option. It is the one thing which God and marriage refuse to allow us. They will not simply let us be. In one way or another they are always on our backs, forever admonishing us that there is no such thing as life apart from relationship, which is to say, no life apart from the sharing of ourselves with another.[7]

Mike Mason

NOTES

1. Matthew Henry, *Commentary on the Whole Bible,* vol. I (Iowa Falls, Iowa: Riverside Book & Bible House, n.d.), page 20.

2. Mike Mason, *The Mystery of Marriage* (Portland, Oreg.: Multnomah Press, 1985), page 47.

3. Charles R. Swindoll, *Strike the Original Match* (Portland, Oreg.: Multnomah Presss, 1980), page 19.

4. Lawrence J. Crabb, Jr., *The Marriage Builder* (Grand Rapids: Zondervan Publishing House, 1982), pages 58-59.

5. Ruth Bell Graham, *It's My Turn* (Old Tappan, N.J.: Fleming H. Revell Company, 1982), page 74.

6. Frank Crane, quoted in *The Marriage Affair,* J. Allan Petersen ed. (Wheaton, Ill.: Tyndale House Publishers, 1971), page 92.

7. Mason, pages 42-43.

"She Brings Him Good, Not Harm"

*Her husband has full
confidence in her and lacks
nothing of value. She brings him
good, not harm, all the days
of her life.*

Proverbs 31:11-12 (NIV)

*The essential foundation for a
biblical marriage relationship is
an unqualified commitment to
the goal of ministry. Each
partner must be willing to
minister to the needs of the other
regardless of the response.
Although all of us will fail to
implement that commitment
perfectly, our responsibility is to
remind ourselves continually
that our highest purpose as
husbands or wives is to be an
instrument for promoting our
partners' spiritual and personal
welfare.*[1]

Lawrence J. Crabb, Jr.

Eve did Adam great harm by encouraging him to eat the forbidden fruit. This pattern of a wife persuading her husband to do what she wants has not diminished since creation. Not only can we be helpers to encourage and promote our husbands, but we can also be wives who dominate and pressure our husbands to their detriment. God prefaced Adam's consequence to sin by saying, "Because you have listened to the voice of your wife" (Genesis 3:17). The influence we have as wives is an area that must be considered and studied. Since we are out of Eden, we must be aware of learning to do our husbands good and not harm all the days of our lives.

Insight into Scripture

1. Eve, tempted by Satan, yielded to sin and then influenced her husband to do the same. What can be learned from this original seduction that can help us today? Read Genesis 3:1-18 and answer the following questions.

   a. Why do you think Satan approached Eve and not Adam?

   b. What main areas of Eve's life did the serpent appeal to?

   c. Write a few sentences explaining Eve's vulnerability to Satan and some ways she could have resisted temptation.

2. The Bible straightforwardly tells the truth about people. Read the verses below and record your observations of how different women influenced or provoked their husbands.

Genesis 16:1-6

Genesis 30:1-2

1 Kings 21:25-26

2 Chronicles 21:5-6

Proverbs 31:10-12

---

3. When God spoke to Eve after the Fall, He said, "Yet your desire shall be for your husband, and he shall rule over you" (Genesis 3:16). Susan Foh interprets this pronouncement, "The 'curse' here describes the beginning of the battle of the sexes. After the fall, the husband no longer rules easily; he must fight for his headship. The woman's desire is to control her husband (to usurp his divinely appointed headship), and he must master her, if he can. Sin has corrupted both the willing submission of the wife and the loving headship of the husband. And so, the rule of love founded in paradise is replaced by struggle, tyranny, domination, and manipulation."[2]

a. How do you see this interpretation exemplified in marriages today?

b. Has this been your experience? Explain.

---

4. In the context of our bent to yield to temptation, read Romans 6:1-14. How does this passage help us to choose to do good?

When Eve succumbed to the tempter's clever argument, Adam proved once and for all, that the creature called *woman* holds within her being a particular power to influence. He proved this by succumbing right along with her! He didn't have to do it. He, too, was a creature with free choice; but the fact remains that he did, leaving us to face another irrevocable fact: that while each human being is morally responsible to God for himself alone, women do have a special responsibility to see to it that their lives influence those around them in a way which God can accept.[3]
Eugenia Price

Insight into myself

5. a. In what ways do I make myself susceptible to temptation?

b. What do I do to encourage myself to be an instrument of righteousness for God?

c. Do I basically influence my husband for his good or my good? Explain.

d. In what areas of our relationship do I tend to control or manipulate my husband?

e. Express your desire to do your husband good and not harm.

> Webster says that manipulation means "to control or play upon by unfair or insidious means, especially to one's own advantage or to serve one's own purpose." In other words, secret manipulation is an unfair, insidious technique that results in getting what one wants. When handled cleverly, a wife can substitute secret manipulation for a quiet, submissive spirit.[4]
> Charles R. Swindoll

Insight into my husband

6. a. How would my husband define the good I do for him?

b. What does my husband consider the evil or harm I might do to him?

c. How does my husband respond when I attempt to control him or try to get my own way?

Insight from an older woman

I have a friend who prays that she will not hinder the will of God in the life of her husband. Eve certainly contributed to Adam's fall, and Sarah influenced Abraham's relationship to Hagar. As we have studied, wives have tremendous opportunity for good or harm.

In order to bring our husbands good, we need to be very close to the Source of goodness. Only as we deepen our intimacy with the Lord are we able to have the wisdom and discernment necessary to do good. Scripture says that the heart is deceitful above all, so we need to guard our hearts with all diligence because what we say and do can influence our husbands. Eve is an example of what happens when we turn away from God and drift into an unguarded situation. (Why was she looking at the fruit anyway?)

It is so natural for me to believe that I know what is best, and it is also easy for me to try to convince Jack that I am right. Our motive should be not to control or pressure our husbands into what we think is right, but to "comfort, encourage and do [them] only good as long as there is life within" us (Proverbs 31:11, AMP).

To satisfy our flesh with unrighteous yet desirable fruit feeds our pride, destroys our intimacy with God, and ensnares those closest to us.
Cynthia Heald

The fear of the LORD is a fountain of life,
That one may avoid the snares of death.
Proverbs 14:27

NOTES
1. Lawrence J. Crabb, Jr., *The Marriage Builder* (Grand Rapids: Zondervan Publishing House, 1982), page 63.
2. Susan T. Foh, *Women and the Word of God: A Response to Biblical Feminism* (Phillipsburg, N.J.: Presbyterian and Reformed Publishing Co., 1979), page 69.
3. Eugenia Price, *God Speaks to Women Today* (Grand Rapids: Zondervan Publishing House, 1964), page 12.
4. Charles R. Swindoll, *Strike the Original Match* (Portland, Oreg.: Multnomah Press, 1980), page 57.

"Let the Wife . . . Respect Her Husband"

*Let the wife see that she respects
and reverences her husband—
that she notices him, regards
him, honors him, prefers him,
venerates and esteems him; and
that she defers to him, praises
him, and loves and admires
him exceedingly.*

Ephesians 5:33 (AMP)

Respect *is shown by giving the
other person freedom to grow
and mature. Respect says,
"You're OK and I admire you
the way you are." Respect
encourages the one loved to be
genuinely himself or herself and
to grow and develop, not for the
sake of serving the spouse, but
simply for his or her own sake.*

Reverence *is an attitude of high
regard for another that contains
no hint of exploitation.*[1]

Josh McDowell

Men tend to have a great need to be respected. The Scriptures clearly state that wives must respect their husbands. Respect means a high or special regard, to esteem, to honor. Some wives feel that they cannot give reverence to their husbands or that their husbands must earn their respect. Most wives accept their husbands, even take them for granted, but they do not actively communicate respect to their husbands. Again, since we are out of Eden, it can be a challenge to venerate and esteem our mates!

Insight into Scripture

1. The beautiful account of Mary anointing the Lord is found in Mark 14:1-9. Read this passage and meditate on the way Mary reverenced Christ. Write down your thoughts.

2. Read 1 Peter 3:1-4. What kind of behavior is to be observed by our husbands? How could this conduct be used of God in the life of a husband?

3. Read Proverbs 31:10-31. In what sense did this excellent wife show her husband respect?

4. a. The Bible faithfully portrays our human frailties. Read the scriptures below and state how these wives were disrespectful to their husbands.

Genesis 27:1-19

Judges 14:15-17

2 Samuel 6:12-23

Hosea 2:5-7

b. Summarize the different ways these wives behaved. Which way challenges you the most in your relationship with your husband?

The way we behave from day to day is largely a function of how we respect or disrespect the people around us. The way employees perform is a product of how they respect the boss. The way children behave is an outgrowth of their respect for their parents. . . . And certainly, the way husbands and wives relate is a function of their mutual respect and admiration. That's why marital discord *almost always* emanates from seething disrespect somewhere in the relationship! That is the *bottom line* of romantic confrontation.[2]

James Dobson

5. a. What are my husband's character qualities that I respect the most?

   b. What aspects of my husband's personality do I not respect?

   c. How do I respond to my husband's qualities or faults that I do not highly esteem?

   d. How can my reverence for Christ begin to encourage my reverence for my husband?

   e. What can I do to deepen my respect for my husband?

   f. How can I specifically begin to show my husband that I respect him?

> In the dream world of mankind's complacent
> separateness, amidst all our pleasant little fantasies of
> omnipotence and blamelessness and self-sufficiency,
> marriage explodes like a bomb. It runs an aggravating
> interference pattern, an unrelenting guerrilla warfare
> against selfishness. It attacks people's vanity and
> lonely pride in a way that few other things can,
> tirelessly exposing the necessity of giving and shar-
> ing, the absurdity of blame. Angering, humiliating,
> melting, chastening, purifying, it touches us where
> we hurt most, in the place of lovelessness.[3]
> Mike Mason

Insight into my husband

6. a. Is my husband confident of my regard for him? Why
or why not?

b. How does my husband respond to my respect and/
or my disrespect of him?

c. In what areas would my husband appreciate more
respect from me?

49

> One of the greatest ministries a wife can have in her
> husband's life is the ministry of encouragement
> through admiration. Not flattery, but sincere praise.[4]
> Carole Mayhall

Insight from an older woman

Respect is a choice of the will. I can choose to focus on my
husband's good qualities and to give him the honor due
him because I did choose him above all others to be my
lifelong mate. I can also choose to esteem my husband
because the Word of God asks me to "see to it" that I do.
The model of my respect is the respect the Church is to
give to Christ. How do I reverence and consider Christ in
my life? This same attitude is to be shared with my
husband.

Many years ago I heard someone ask the question,
"Do you know what makes a leader?" The answer was
simply "a follower." When I examined my life (independent as I am) I found myself—as Sarah's daughter—running
ahead of Jack (and the Lord). I was not allowing Jack to
lead or giving him the support and respect he needed to
be the head of our home. Some ways I tended to show disrespect for him were to challenge his decisions and, more
often than not, to offer my alternatives to those decisions.
I would interrupt and correct him in front of others, especially in front of the children. In my effort to inspire him to
be his very best, I would give him my lecture entitled,
"Whatever you do, it's just not good enough." He could be
home more, he could spend more time with the children,
he could read more, he could be more sensitive, he could
be more spiritual.

One day it dawned on me that I was not Jack's personal
Holy Spirit. My job was to respect him and to fulfill *my*
God-given role in our marriage. I was not given to Jack to
redo him, but to complement him. When I finally became
aware of the log in my eye, I was able to back off and begin
to give him time and encouragement to lead. He, then,

slowly but confidently became the head of our home.

I have learned that as I respect Jack, I am not so inclined to manipulate him. *My* respect for Jack was necessary to free him to be the husband and father he was meant to be.

> Do not withhold good from those to whom it is due,
> When it is in your power to do it.
> Proverbs 3:27

NOTES
1. Josh McDowell, *The Secret of Loving* (Wheaton, Ill.: Tyndale House Publishers, 1985), pages 262-263.
2. James Dobson, *Love Must Be Tough* (Waco, Tex.: Word Books Publisher, 1983), pages 44-45.
3. Mike Mason, *The Mystery of Marriage* (Portland, Oreg.: Multnomah Press, 1985), page 45.
4. Carole Mayhall, "Choosing to Admire," in *Marriage Takes More Than Love,* by Jack and Carole Mayhall (Colorado Springs, Colo.: NavPress, 1978), page 150.

"To Love Their Husbands"

Then [the older women] can train the younger women to love their husbands and children.

Titus 2:4 (NIV)

Next to the love of God, the "one thing" that is by far the most important in the life of all married people is their marriage, their loving devotion to their partner. Nothing on earth must take precedence over that, not children, jobs, other friendships, nor even "Christian work."[1]

Mike Mason

Paul writes to Titus that older women are to teach younger women how to love their husbands. It is interesting that we, as women, are to be instructed in how to properly love our husbands! God wants us to be equipped especially through the teaching of older women. This can be done, not only personally, but from books, tapes, and studies. The Greek word *philandros* is used to express "loving one's husband." It is from the root word phileō, which means to show affection, love, devotion, hospitality.[2] It speaks of being fond of friends and relatives. Therefore, we are to be taught to love our husbands as companions and good friends!

Insight into Scripture

1. a. The following verses exhort us to love. Read these scriptures and write down the key thought of each passage.

   Matthew 22:34-40

   John 13:34

   Galatians 5:22-23

   1 Thessalonians 4:9-10

   1 Peter 1:22

b. How do these verses encourage you to love your husband?

---

2. We are commanded to love our neighbor (our husband is our nearest neighbor!) as we love ourselves. The source of our love for others is important.

   a. Read 1 John 4:7-21. Write down the key observations given about love in this passage.

   b. What are the basic truths in these verses that can also apply to the marriage relationship?

---

3. Any study on love must consider 1 Corinthians 13:1-7. The Greek word used in these verses is *agape*, which expresses unselfish esteem for the object loved, not just mutual affection.[3] Study Paul's description of love and write down how each of the aspects of love can

guide you specifically in deepening your love and
friendship with your husband.

4. Ephesians 3:14-19 is a beautiful prayer concerning
   being rooted and grounded in love. Read these verses
   and write down the main petitions. Pray this prayer for
   yourself as a wife. (You might also pray this prayer for
   your husband.)

And so the best marriages and the deepest relationships with God grow out of the startling discovery
that there is nothing one can do to earn love, and
even more startling, that there is also nothing one can
do to un-earn it, or to keep oneself from being loved.
This is a religious awakening that is utterly different
from any other religious experience, no matter how
profoundly spiritual it may seem. It is the recognition
of the true self in the simple discovery that one is
loved. "How beautiful you are, my darling! Oh, how
beautiful!" say the words of the fourth chapter of the
Song of Songs. "You have stolen my heart with one
glance of your eyes." They are the words of God Himself speaking personally, with outrageous intimacy, to
every human soul.[4]

Mike Mason

Insight into myself

5. a. How do I know that God loves me?

b. In what ways do I draw upon the love of God in order to love as I should?

c. Do I consider my husband a good friend? Why?

d. In what ways do I communicate love and friendship to my husband?

e. How is my love for my husband evident to other people?

f. From studying 1 Corinthians 13 what is my greatest area of need in loving my husband?

g. What can I begin to do to deepen my love for my husband?

> Love can be expressed through patience, tolerance for the failings of your husband, meeting his needs, and by avoiding criticism. Love does not demand, it gives. Your own need for love can make you unlovable if it is expressed in a demanding or martyred manner. . . . Marriage is the most difficult and complex of all human relationships, and it requires patience, skill, tact, and emotional and spiritual growth. You can "grow a good marriage" if you are willing to work at it.[5]
>
> Cecil Osborne

Insight into my husband

6. a. How would my husband define love?

b. Does my husband consider me a good friend? Why?

c. How would my husband respond if I asked him, "What is one thing I do that hurts you?"

d. In what way would my husband like me "to excel still more" in my love for him?

The apostle Paul didn't say that love bears some things, that love believes only in the best things, that love hopes for a reasonable period of time, or that it endures for a while. No, love is a divine absurdity. It is unreasonable. Paul said, "Love bears all things, believes all things, hopes all things, endures all things." Love is limitless. For-give-ness is to give infinitely, without end.[6]

Walter Wangerin, Jr.

Insight from an older woman

It encouraged me to know that wives are to relate to and love their husbands as friends. Spiritual, *agape* love is foundational, but in marriage we are also to enjoy one another as friends. In their book, *Friends and Friendship*, Jerry and Mary White define a friend as "loyal, one who shares deeply, fun, stimulating, encouraging, self-sacrificing, loving, and spiritually challenging."[7] A pretty good definition of a godly wife!

It is so easy to settle into roles, routines, and ruts in marriage. So often Jack and I are both tired in the evening and have little to give to one another because we have been giving to others (children included). Just as we schedule specific times to be with other friends, it is also necessary to plan time to be with our husbands.

For years I didn't think I should take the initiative to arrange any special times for us to be together. Finally, one day it dawned on me that I was the creative one in our relationship and it was all right for me to make suggestions and plans for our time together. (It was also a relief to Jack!) Our times together have included crackers and cheese after the children were in bed to relaxing weekends away.

It is in these special times that we can express our love and deepen its growth. A friend delights in planning and doing thoughtful things for loved ones. What kind of friend are you to your husband?

The Scriptures describe a giving love—a love that says, "Whatever I have, I want to share with you, and I want you to be what God meant you to be." It is a love that takes first things first as far as the other person is concerned. We can see immediately that this kind of love is not emotional. One does not fall into and then out of this kind of love. It is a love of the will. It is something addressed to our volition. We do it because we make ourselves do it. We order ourselves. Because of Christ, we are motivated to love. We do not wait for attraction or like interests.[8]

Arthur H. DeKruyter

NOTES
1. Mike Mason, *The Mystery of Marriage* (Portland, Oreg.: Multnomah Press, 1985), page 99.
2. From *The New International Dictionary of New Testament Theology,* Colin Brown ed., vol. II (Grand Rapids: Zondervan Publishing House, 1986), pages 547, 549.
3. From a reference note on 1 Corinthians 13:1 in *The Ryrie Study Bible: New American Standard Translation,* Charles Caldwell Ryrie ed. (Chicago: Moody Press, 1978), page 1744.
4. Mason, pages 63-64.
5. Cecil Osborne, "When the Honeymoon Is Over," in *The Marriage Affair,* J. Allan Petersen ed. (Wheaton, Ill.: Tyndale House Publishers, 1971), page 98.
6. Walter Wangerin, Jr., *As for Me and My House: Crafting Your Marriage to Last* (Nashville: Thomas Nelson Publishers, 1987), page 81.
7. Jerry and Mary White, *Friends and Friendship* (Colorado Springs, Colo.: Nav-Press, 1982), page 31.
8. Arthur H. DeKruyter, in *Family Concern,* J. Allan Petersen ed., vol. 10, no. 3 (1986).

"Wives . . . Be Submissive"

Wives be subject—be submissive and adapt yourselves—to your own husbands as [a service] to the Lord.

Ephesians 5:22 (AMP)

The submission of the wife to her husband is not that of an inferior to a superior. The woman is joint heir (with the man) of God's promises; she, like the man, bears the image of God and as a Christian will be conformed to Christ's image. The different roles husband and wife have are by God's appointment and design. That the woman and man are equal in being is re-enforced by the command to wives. Wives are to submit themselves *(reflexive); their submission is voluntary, self-imposed. It is part of their obedience to the Lord; the Lord is the one who commands it, not the husband.*[1]

Susan T. Foh

LESSON 7

Submission has been defined as yielding intelligent, humble obedience to an ordained authority. There are many common misconceptions, and therefore submission needs to be prayerfully studied and understood. God has asked us, as wives, to submit to a man we chose and most likely did our best to attract. As Christian wives in today's world—which idealizes the independent, self-oriented woman—we must consider biblical submission in depth.

Insight into Scripture

1. Submission is, more than anything else, an attitude. Nowhere in Scripture is this more beautifully portrayed than in Philippians 2:5-16. Read these verses and answer the following questions.

   a. Define *attitude.*

   b. What attitude did Christ have?

   c. How did Christ exemplify this attitude?

   d. In verses 12-16, what encouragement and instructions are written for our exercise of humility?

   e. How does this whole passage speak to you concerning your submissive attitude in general?

2. In the context of Christ as our example of submission, consider the teaching on submission found in Ephesians 5:22 and Colossians 3:18. Study the surrounding verses carefully to help you understand these key commands.

    a. Read Ephesians 5:15-24 and Colossians 3:12-17. What key instructions are given in these passages to all believers?

    b. If these instructions were followed how would these scriptures promote a submissive attitude in a godly wife?

3. Peter addresses all relationships that need respectful submission, especially a Christian wife married to a husband who is not obedient to the Word. Read 1 Peter 2:11-3:17 and respond to the following questions.

    a. What kind of behavior are we to have among unbelievers? Why?

    b. To what different authorities is submission commanded?

c. What scriptural reasons and examples are given to keep submitting even when suffering is involved (2:15-3:2)?

d. Read 1 Peter 3:8-17 from the perspective that these verses are specific truths for a wife living in a difficult marriage, or going through a difficult time in her marriage. Summarize your thoughts.

---

4. Does submission mean doing or agreeing with everything your husband decides? Read the scriptural example of Sapphira in Acts 5:1-11 and answer the following questions.

a. What were the circumstances concerning Ananias and Sapphira?

b. Write your thoughts about Sapphira's individual responsibility before God and her role as a helper to her husband.

c. How does this example contribute to your understanding of biblical submission?

---

5. a. Characterize the relationship the following women
had with their husbands.

Samson's mother—Judges 13 (note verse 23)

Shunamite woman—2 Kings 4:8-24 (note verses
10,22-23; see verses 25-37 to finish the story)

Priscilla—Acts 18:24-26

b. What can be learned from these women about relating to our husbands?

Before your feathers get ruffled by what this says of Sarah ("obeyed"), it will help you to realize the Greek verb means "to pay close attention to" some-one. It's the idea of attending to the needs of another. A positive, helpful response is written between these lines.[2]

Charles R. Swindoll

Insight into myself

6. a. What problems, if any, do I have in submitting to ordained authorities? Why?

b. What fears keep me from biblically submitting to my husband?

c. Is a submissive attitude part of my lifestyle? Why or why not?

d. What specific encouragement have I received from the Scriptures to help me submit properly to my husband?

The Christian wife has the responsibility to grow in Christ, to know doctrine, to be able to speak the truth in love. That is, she is not to be ignorant, nor to rely on her husband's knowledge and/or participation as a substitute for her own. In addition, she is not to be silent when her husband sins (Matt. 18:15), but she is to teach and admonish him (Col. 3:16). However, she is to do all these things with a submissive heart. Her submission manifests itself in lowliness, meekness, patience, forbearance in love, and eagerness to maintain the unity of the Spirit in the bond of peace (Eph. 4:2-3) but also in reverence for her husband as her head. The Christian wife is neither passive nor mindless. She does not have to pretend her husband is always right or hide her own talents or intelligence. She is to use her gifts for the upbuilding of the body of Christ, which includes her husband.[3]

Susan T. Foh

Insight into my husband

7. a. Does my husband sense my submissive spirit? Why or why not?

b. How does my submission contribute to my husband's sense of adequacy?

> All of Scripture is for wives. All of the Bible is for every Christian. Scriptures such as "speak the truth in love" and "admonish one another daily" are totally compatible with being a wife who is in submission to her husband. Submission is an attitude of *heart*. . . and an attitude of yieldedness and of love.[4]
> Carole Mayhall

Insight from an older woman

Submission is the lifestyle of any consecrated Christian. Part of the freedom that Christ offers is the freedom from self-protection and self-promotion. Secure in Christ, one is able to be vulnerable and to minister to others, especially to a spouse. Deference and mutual submission are to be practiced in the Body of Christ. God, in His plan, has specifically asked wives, however, to submit to their husbands. This submission is the Lord's direction, and we need to trust that what God has ordained is right and good. God would not ask us to be in a position where His grace and strength were not sufficient and where His will would not be perfect.

Submission is a willing adaptation; a voluntary selflessness to please God and to obey His Word. This submission is not blind; it is a conscious choice of the will in keeping with scriptural truth. Larry Crabb defined submission as resisting the urge to control. A major part of that, he added, is to keep entrusting yourself to God.

Some women submit outwardly, but not inwardly. Some wives submit in order to manipulate. Others submit out of weakness, not out of strength in Christ. Submission goes hand in hand with respect. A wife needs to be willing to minister to her husband's sense of adequacy, and only submission that is sincere and biblical will do that. The Scriptures are careful to tell us to submit to our own husbands. Therefore, submission cannot be standardized or compared from one couple to another. In its application, it is highly unique to each relationship.

Women legitimately ask if there are limits to submission. Susan Foh wrote, "The wife's submission to her husband is qualified by God's commands, not her own preferences, opinions, or even expertise."[5] When questions arise from a pure heart, a wife needs to pray for wisdom and discernment and, if necessary, seek godly counsel.

Charles Swindoll addressed the need for prayer and counsel particularly in critical circumstances:

> It is one thing to be in subjection. It is another thing entirely to become the brunt of indignity, physical assault, sexual perversion, and uncontrolled rage. . . . At such crisis times, call for help! Seek out a Christian friend who can assist you. Talk with your pastor or a competent counselor who will provide both biblical guidance and emotional support. And pray! Pray that your Lord will bring about changes in the unbearable circumstances surrounding you. Ask for deliverance, safety, stability, and great grace to see you through, to settle your fears, to calm your spirit so you can think and act responsibly.[6]

It is important for us to be sure that our submission is biblical. Submission should be done for the right reason so it will accomplish God's intended purpose for marriage. Here are some fundamental guidelines I have written to help determine biblical submission.

Guidelines for Biblical Submission

● Submission is an attitude exemplified by a voluntary yielding of rights.

● Submission springs from a position of security and strength in who we are in Christ.

● Submission should uphold our integrity before God.

● Submission is discerned through abiding in Christ and His Word.

● The goal of submission is to obey God and glorify Him.

> Strength and dignity are her clothing,
> And she smiles at the future.
> Proverbs 31:25

NOTES

1. Susan T. Foh, *Women and the Word of God: A Response to Biblical Feminism* (Phillipsburg, N.J.: Presbyterian and Reformed Publishing Co., 1979), page 186.
2. Charles R. Swindoll, *Strike the Original Match* (Portland, Oreg.: Multnomah Press, 1980), page 49.
3. Foh, page 186.
4. Carole Mayhall, "Choosing to Submit," in *Marriage Takes More Than Love* (Colorado Springs, Colo.: NavPress, 1978), page 191.
5. Foh, page 184.
6. Swindoll, page 159.

"For I Have Learned to Be Content"

*For I have learned to be content
in whatever circumstances I am.*
Philippians 4:11

*Christian contentment is that
sweet, inward, quiet, gracious
frame of spirit, which freely
submits to and delights in God's
wise and fatherly disposal in
every condition.*[1]
Jeremiah Burroughs

Solomon, who had three hundred wives, wrote, "Better is a dry morsel and quietness with it, than a house full of feasting with strife" (Proverbs 17:1). Luxurious surroundings cannot begin to compensate for contention and strife in a home. It is interesting that a contentious woman is frequently mentioned in Proverbs. Apparently, a husband would rather endure great hardship than live with a quarrelsome wife! What motivates a wife to be argumentative? What is an antidote to contentiousness?

Insight into Scripture

1. Using a dictionary or thesaurus, define the words below. If possible, record several synonyms for each word.

   content—

   contentious—

   strife—

2. Often Scripture is very direct and descriptive. Read the following verses and write a paragraph explaining the truth found in these Proverbs: 21:19, 25:24, 27:15.

3. a. What reasons for contention and strife are given in the following verses?

Proverbs 10:12

Proverbs 13:10

Proverbs 15:18

Proverbs 20:3

Proverbs 28:25

James 4:1-6

b. What impressed you most about the causes of contentiousness?

4. One definition of *content* is "not disposed to complain or grumble." This makes a contented wife the antithesis of a contentious wife. Read 2 Corinthians 12:7-10 and Philippians 4:10-13. What insights on contentment can be gained from Paul's experiences?

5. Read the verses below and write down the specific areas of our lives in which contentment is to be practiced.

Luke 3:14

1 Timothy 6:6-10

Hebrews 13:5

Godliness does not give financial gain; it itself is gain when accompanied with *contentment. Autarkeias* literally means "self-sufficiency." Yet the sufficiency of oneself is due to the sufficiency of God. Godliness combined with that inner God-given sufficiency which does not depend on material circumstances is indeed of great gain.[2]

A. Duane Liftin

---

6. Job—stripped of his children, possessions, and health—sits on an ash heap desperately questioning his life and circumstances. In the midst of his suffering, consider the words of his wife found in Job 2:9-10.

a. What do you think motivated Job's wife to say these words to her husband?

b. Write down what a wife whose security and trust are in God would say to Job.

Every human being is subject to moods, and women by no means have a corner on this instability of temperament. There are some moods which are peculiar to women, though, and we have the reputation of being inconsistent and variable in our emotions. We have moods with pregnancy, moods with menopause, and then, just to keep things humming, in between we have moods that are directly related to our monthly menstrual periods. . . . Of course, all moods are not due to pre-menstrual tension. . . . When you are caught in the grip of a mood, go stand before the Lord, and [like Elijah] stay there, until the storm passes over and you hear the still small voice of God.[3]

Shirley Rice

Insight into myself

7. a. When I am contentious, what prompts or motivates me to be quarrelsome?

b. What do I feel?

c. What do I want?

d. Is what I want consistent with what God wants for me? Explain.

e. As a Christian, what are my choices?

---

8. Am I content with my husband? (Have I accepted him for just who he is—imperfections and all?) Why or why not?

---

9. When David was contentious and angry because someone had caused him great strife and hurt, he wrote down his feelings to God. (Psalm 55 and 109 are good examples.) In my Bible by Psalm 55:16-17, I have written the words, "The Complaint Department." When we need to complain and murmur, where are we to go? The Lord wants us to come before Him in honesty, telling Him everything. This must be done frequently.

Perhaps with pen in hand you can take time now to "pour out your heart to God." He knows your thoughts, but it is important that you acknowledge them to Him.

In taking our complaints to God, we gain release, perspective, and strength—perhaps it will keep us from sounding like constantly dripping rain!

10. What are some specific ways and in what particular areas can I begin to *learn* contentment?

> The refusal to be disillusioned is the cause of much of the suffering in human life. It works in this way—if we love a human being and do not love God, we demand of him every perfection and every rectitude, and when we do not get it we become cruel and vindictive; we are demanding of a human being that which he or she cannot give. There is only one Being Who can satisfy the last aching abyss of the human heart, and that is the Lord Jesus Christ.[4]
> Oswald Chambers

Insight into my husband

11. a. In what area would my husband say I am most likely to be quarrelsome?

b. In what area would my husband say I am most likely to be discontent (e.g.: finances, possessions, his work, etc.)?

c. How does my husband respond to my contentiousness?

d. Would my husband say that I am content with him? Why or why not?

> They never felt God's love or tasted forgiveness of sins who are discontented.[5]
> Richard Greenham

Insight from an older woman

If Jack were a contemporary Soloman, a proverb I'm sure he would write is, "It is better to walk alone than ride in a car with a contentious woman." I don't know why I feel that I have to direct, control, and critique his driving! I understand that contentious in the Greek means "umpire." That is exactly what I often become in Jack's life. How lovely to live with an umpire who never goes off duty!

Essentially, I am contentious because Jack (or anyone else) isn't doing what I think should be done in the way I would do it. In others words, I'm not getting my way. I am not in control! When I create dissension, my purpose is to control and to change the person or circumstances: i.e. my husband or the situation is unacceptable.

I am learning later in life that I tend to be contentious about things that wouldn't matter two hours later, or I'm quick to find fault with Jack's decisions and ideas. I am not actually helping my husband by nagging him or quarreling with him about his choices. I am not ministering to my husband by demanding that he perform according to my specific plan for his life.

I *can* share honestly, in a godly manner, my feelings and thoughts. I can exercise self-control in my responses. I can do all things through Christ who strengthens me and gives my life the only basis for contentment.

> An excellent wife is the crown of her husband,
> But she who shames him is as rottenness in
> his bones.
>
> Proverbs 12:4

NOTES

1. Jeremiah Burroughs, *The Rare Jewel of Christian Contentment* (London: Banner of Truth Trust, 1648, 1964), page 5.
2. A. Duane Litfin in *The Bible Knowledge Commentary,* John F. Walvoord and Roy B. Zuck eds., New Testament Edition (Wheaton, Ill.: Victor Books, 1983), page 246.
3. Shirley Rice, *The Christian Home: A Woman's View* (Norfolk, Va.: The Tabernacle Church of Norfolk, 1965), pages 49, 52-53.
4. Oswald Chambers, *My Utmost for His Highest* (New York: Dodd, Mead & Company, 1935), page 212.
5. Richard Greenham, quoted in *The Treasury of David,* by Charles H. Spurgeon, vol. I (McLean, Va.: MacDonald Publishing Co., n.d.), pages 195-196.

"Let No Unwholesome Word Proceed from Your Mouth"

Let no unwholesome word proceed from your mouth, but only such a word as is good for edification according to the need of the moment, that it may give grace to those who hear.

Ephesians 4:29

For the tongue is a pen, which pressing deeply enough (and whether for good or for evil) will write upon the heart.[1]

Mike Mason

"Workshops on communication teach verbal strategies for sharing and listening in nonattacking and nondefensive styles, but they rarely pinpoint the key problem of selfish motivation. Sharing and listening skills are important to learn, but I rather think that the effort spent teaching the skills could sometimes be better used to persuade people to stop living self-centered lives and to seek first the purposes of God."[2] With these thoughts Larry Crabb diagnoses the fundamental problem of communication in marriage. We can learn helpful skills in communicating, but until our hearts are freed from self and focused on pleasing God, we will not experience truly intimate communication.

Insight into Scripture

1. The root word for communication is *commune*, which means to converse or confer intimately. Carefully read Ephesians 4:20-32 in the context of pleasing God with our communication and answer the following questions.

   a. What is involved in putting on the new self, and how can the new self help in communicating in the right way (verses 20-24)?

   b. Your husband is your nearest neighbor. What can you learn from verse 25 about communicating with him?

   c. What instructions do verses 26-27 provide for communicating negative feelings?

d. What guidelines for conversation can you find in verses 29-30?

e. According to verse 31, what must we put away from our lives in order to speak the truth in love? How can we do this?

f. What is the final admonition in verse 32? Why is it important in communication?

Forgiveness is a willing relinquishment of certain rights. The one sinned against chooses *not* to demand her rights of redress for the hurt she has suffered. She does not hold her spouse accountable for his sin, nor enforce a punishment upon him, nor exact a payment from him, as in "reparations." She does not make his life miserable in order to balance accounts for her own misery, though she might feel perfectly justified in doing so, tit for tat: "He deserves to be hurt as he hurt me." In this way (please note this carefully) she steps outside the systems of law; she steps into the world of mercy. She makes possible a whole new economy for their relationship: not the cold-blooded and killing machinery of rules, rights, and privileges, but the tender and nourishing care of mercy, which always rejoices in the growth, not the guilt or the pain, of the other. This is sacrifice. To give up one's rights is to sacrifice something of one's self— something hard-fought-for in the world.[3]
Walter Wangerin, Jr.

2. List the truths for being a good communicator found in the verses below.

   Matthew 12:34-35

   Galatians 6:1

   James 1:19-26

   James 4:1

   1 Peter 2:21-23

---

3. Esther, a Jew, was married to a Persian king who had signed a decree to have all the Jews killed. She was in a unique and life-threatening situation, for which she needed great courage and wisdom. In her response, she provides a beautiful model for all of us of how to approach a husband who might be making a decision or has made a decision that we feel before God is not right.

   a. What was the first thing Esther did (4:16)?

   b. What did Esther prepare for her husband (5:4)? Why do you think she chose to do this?

c. Even though her husband asked Esther to share what she wanted, why do you think she waited until the next day to tell him?

d. What basic principles of marital communication can we learn from Esther's example?

Even before you face your spouse, it is absolutely necessary that you pause and self-consciously surrender the world and all its rights. You drop legalities. You die. Can you in fact do this on your own? Not often and never well. Only Jesus purely whispered from the cross, "Father, forgive them, for they know not what they do." Therefore, it is Jesus who must love you in this step. It is Jesus who frees you from yourself, emptying you of your own will even as once he emptied himself. It is Jesus who divorces you, not from your spouse but from the law, to place you fully under his light of grace. Here your faith, shaped by serious prayer, comes to life, for this is done in trust alone; this is Christ's act and will therefore reveal Christ in your actions. You will demand of your spouse nothing for yourself. Anger has vanished from you; vengeance is gone; love alone is left.[4]
Walter Wangerin, Jr.

Insight into myself

4. a. Are there any obstacles in my heart that I need to lay aside in order to communicate as I should with my

husband? If so, what are they and what do I need to do to remove them?

b. Do I have a "rein on my tongue"? If not, what can I do to begin to bridle my tongue?

c. Can honest prayer become a vital part of my life? How can I ensure that prayer is a priority?

d. How can I instruct my husband to tell me, in an acceptable way, when I hurt or nag him by my speech or actions?

Prolonged anger can kill a marriage—especially when it reflects perceived wrongs from the past that have never been forgiven. Thus, the *love must be tough* concept does not suggest that people become touchy and picky; it *does* hold that genuine instances of disrespect should be acknowledged and handled within the context of love.[5]

James Dobson

Insight into my husband

5. a. Does my husband feel free to talk with me? Why or why not?

b. Does my husband consider me a good listener? Why or why not?

c. How would I describe my husband's communication style?

d. Have I accepted or understood my husband's way of communicating? Why or why not?

e. How would my husband want me to change in the way I communicate with him?

Because many husband and wives see no evidence that their ministry can be meaningful to their partners, it is essential that they develop an awareness of their spouse's deepest needs. We can create a climate of noncritical acceptance to encourage our spouses to risk becoming vulnerable. If our partners will not open up, we must realize that because they are made in God's image, deep needs do exist, even if they are well hidden. We must pray for wisdom to know what to do to touch those needs.[6]

Lawrence J. Crabb, Jr.

Insight from an older woman

I cringe remembering how often I criticize, interrupt, or correct Jack. I tend to believe that Jack can take it. He knows I really love him, so I take "short-cuts" in my communication with him. Too easily I jump to conclusions or assume I know what he is going to say. It is hard for me to lay aside the old self: "I'm right"; "That's stupid!"; "Why did you decide that?"; "I can't believe you forgot this!"

Recognizing my critical spirit is a great rebuke to what dwells in my heart—self and all that feeds it. How important to remember that the source of conflict springs from my selfish desires.

The heart of the husband of the Proverbs 31 woman trusted her. I think one reason he could trust her was that when he talked or shared his thoughts, she really listened. She didn't put him down or lecture him. I feel that she created an atmosphere where her husband felt comfortable in answering her questions and in sharing his plans and decisions. "She opens her mouth in wisdom, and the teaching of kindness is on her tongue" (Proverbs 31:26). She was probably quick to listen and slow to speak!

Esther perfectly illustrates being slow to speak. Her discipline of fasting (prayer undoubtedly was the purpose of her fast) before confronting her husband is a good example for us. I think the length of prayer and fasting would be in proportion to the seriousness of what you needed to share.

The main lesson to learn here is to *pray first* and be spiritually attuned to the Holy Spirit before confronting or sharing negative feelings. Only the Holy Spirit can prepare our husband's heart, and only the Holy Spirit can prompt us with the right time, the right way, and the right words. Sometimes after concentrated prayer, our hearts will be changed and there will not even be a need to share.

Fasting is a spiritual discipline that focuses on feeding our spirits and not our bodies. It enables us to be strengthened inwardly and to seek the Lord's will for us wholeheartedly. I recommend a partial fast that eliminates food, but not liquids, and lasts only during the daylight hours for only one day. I personally feel that specific prayer (and fasting as needed) is excellent for receiving strength and much-needed wisdom and direction.

Many wives feel that no matter what they do, their husbands seldom want to communicate. Again, prayer can help us in understanding our husbands and in guiding us in how to relate to them. Also helpful is reading books on marriage to gain insight into our husbands. The bottom line in communication is simply the willingness to minister unconditionally. This ministry can be defined by . . .

- speaking the truth with him in love and kindness;
- listening to him sacrificially with patience and gentleness;
- guarding what he says with faithfulness;
- responding to him with goodness and self-control;
- communing with him in joy;
- being silent with him in peace.

Don't think that friendship authorizes you to say disagreeable things to your intimates. The nearer you come into relation with a person, the more necessary do tact and courtesy become.[7]
Oliver Wendell Holmes

NOTES

1. Mike Mason, *The Mystery of Marriage* (Portland, Oreg.: Multnomah Press, 1985), page 67.
2. Lawrence J. Crabb. Jr., *The Marriage Builder* (Grand Rapids: Zondervan Publishing House, 1982), page 64.
3. Walter Wangerin, Jr., *As for Me and My House: Crafting Your Marriage to Last* (Nashville: Thomas Nelson Publishers, 1987), pages 79-80.
4. Wangerin, pages 99-100.
5. James Dobson, *Love Must Be Tough* (Waco, Tex.: Word Books Publisher, 1983), page 89.
6. Crabb, page 60.
7. Oliver Wendell Holmes, quoted in *The Marriage Affair,* J. Allan Petersen ed. (Wheaton, Ill.: Tyndale House Publishers, 1971), page 368.

"They Shall Become One Flesh"

Therefore a man shall leave his father and his mother and shall become united and cleave to his wife, and they shall become one flesh. . . . And the man and his wife were both naked, and were not embarrassed or ashamed in each other's presence.

Genesis 2:24-25 (AMP)

God created this one-flesh experience to be the most intense height of physical intimacy and the most profound depth of spiritual oneness between husband and wife.[1]

Herbert J. Miles

"Since the world views sex so sordidly and perverts and exploits it so persistently and since so many marriages are crumbling because of lack of love, commitment, and devotion, it is advantageous to have a book in the Bible that gives God's endorsement of marital love as wholesome and pure."[2] So wrote Jack S. Deere about the Song of Solomon. This beautiful book has been interpreted as an allegory, a drama, a lyric poem, a historical record, and a loving illustration of God's relationship with His people. The uniqueness of Scripture is that it is fathomless—and this song, particularly, communicates not only on a spiritual level but also on a practical, human level. The Song of Solomon, along with other scriptures, speaks beautifully and specifically about sex in marriage.

Insight into Scripture

1. In the Song of Solomon God commends to husband and wife the unique intimacy provided by the physical relationship. Take time to read this poetical book carefully (find a translation that outlines the verses by telling who is speaking and what is taking place). As you read, look for some of the key ways the Shulammite woman expresses her love for her beloved in the following areas:

   a. In her personal thoughts—

   b. Verbally to her beloved—

c. To her friends/the daughters of Jerusalem—

d. What can you learn from these expressions of love and intimacy about relating to your husband in your physical relationship?

---

2. What does this book teach us about God's view of the sexual relationship? (Look up Hebrews 13:4 as a helpful cross-reference.)

---

3. a. God's original design and intent for the one flesh relationship is found in Genesis 2:21-25. Read these verses and comment on why Adam and Eve were both naked and yet were not ashamed.

b. What do you think hinders us today from experiencing this kind of freedom in the marriage relationship?

> Still, though banished from Eden, the first couple
> were not banished from one another's arms, nor from
> the marriage bed. This is one garden to which God
> continues to welcome husbands and wives, and
> where they are privileged to return again and again in
> order to expose their nakedness and to be healed of
> secrecy and separateness.[3]
>
> Mike Mason

4. The physical dimension enhances marriage in many
   ways. Read the following scriptures and write down
   what is suggested about the ministry of an intimate
   relationship.

   Genesis 18:11-14

   Genesis 24:67

   2 Samuel 12:24 (see verses 18-24 for context)

5. The Scriptures clearly instruct a husband and wife in
   how to relate to one another sexually. Read 1 Corinthians 7:1-5 and consider the following questions.

   a. Whose responsibility is it to meet whose needs?

   b. In what sense is mutual consideration important
      for the physical relationship?

c. What conditions are mentioned for refraining from sexual intercourse?

God steps boldly to the point, finishing any faint-hearted commitment to the sexual relationship once and for all. My body is not mine, but my mate's. I am here to please. Hereafter, to demand rights over my body is to disagree with God's instruction. God makes sex a sacrificial act that is redemptive, in that it gets my eyes off my needs and onto the needs of my mate.[4]

Don Meredith

Insight into myself

6. a. What words describe my current attitudes toward the physical relationship in my marriage?

b. In what ways do I practice or am I willing to practice God's design for sex in our marriage?

c. In what ways am I reluctant to follow God's design, and why?

d. How can I begin to deepen my enjoyment of the one-flesh relationship with my husband?

Have you misused your sexual relationship in the past? Have you used sex as a tool of manipulation or as a weapon against your husband? Have you rejected him on a whim? Have you withheld physical favors to get even with him? Have you been dishonest with him, playing games? Have you battered his sexuality through hostility or criticism or ridicule?

You should realize that your husband is psychologically vulnerable to injury in the area of sex just as he is physically vulnerable to injury. If you have damaged his sense of manhood and participated in producing an attitude of failure within him, you will have to start all over again and build him up by your tenderness, your sensitivity, your respect, and your responsiveness.[5]

Ed Wheat

Insight into my husband

7. a. How does my husband view me as a sex partner?

b. How might I deepen my husband's enjoyment of our physical relationship?

Talk truthfully, without a hint of guilt or else of criticism, even about sexual difficulties . . . talk as partners who are discussing the third being between you—as parents would discuss a child in need of special care. Then all your talk will be positive, a building up and not a tearing down. It isn't a baby, of course; it's your sex life. But speaking this way, you will be able to handle even heavy things (impotence, frigidity, genital pain, unexpected feelings of anger) without focusing guilt on one or shame on the other—which would divide and silence you after all, and would perpetuate the problem between you. Parents talk very well to share the work of healing a sick child, because together they love that child. Spouses likewise can talk openly, and share their talents, their perceptions, opinions, and their actions to heal a troubled sex life—because together they possess that life.[6]

Walter Wangerin, Jr.

Insight from an older woman

I would like to offer three considerations that have helped me grow in my physical relationship with Jack. The first is a continuous, deepening desire to please God with all of my life. If this is truly my motivation, then I must allow the Holy Spirit and His Word to prompt me to obedience and creativity in this area. We are to do all that we do to the glory of God.

The second is my being willing to talk with Jack about our sex life. It has helped tremendously for us to verbalize our feelings concerning the joys and pleasures of our being together, but it has also helped for us to share our disappointments and frustrations over raised expectations and hurtful responses. The ability to talk about our love-making has been a major step in our growth together.

The third consideration is the benefit of reading Christian books on the physical relationship. There are godly men and women who can instruct, encourage, and share in a biblical way about sex in marriage. Several excellent books are: *Intended for Pleasure,* by Ed and Gaye Wheat; *The Act of Marriage,* by Tim LaHaye; *Solomon on Sex,* by Joseph Dillow; *Sexual Happiness in Marriage,* by Herbert Miles; and *The Gift of Sex,* by Cliff and Joyce Penner.

As I have gotten older and grown in understanding and enjoyment of the one-flesh relationship, this act of marriage has increased my awe, my appreciation, and my obedience to our loving Creator. Truly, we are fearfully and wonderfully made!

For women sex is only one means of intimacy out of many and not always the best one. For many men, sex is the only expression of intimacy.

Men tend to compress the meaning of intimacy into the sex act and when they don't have that outlet, they can become frustrated and upset. Why? Because they're cut off from the only source of closeness they know. Men are interested in closeness and intimacy but they have different ways of defining and expressing it. Here again is an area where men and women need to talk, listen, understand the other person's view of sex and in some way learn to speak the other person's language.[7]

H. Norman Wright

NOTES

1. Herbert J. Miles, *Sexual Happiness in Marriage* (Grand Rapids: Zondervan Publishing House, 1967), page 28.
2. Jack S. Deere in *The Bible Knowledge Commentary,* J.F. Walvoord and R.B. Zuck eds., Old Testament Edition (Wheaton, Ill.: Victor Press, 1985), page 1010.
3. Mike Mason, *The Mystery of Marriage* (Portland, Oreg.: Multnomah Press, 1985), page 118.
4. Don Meredith, *Becoming One: Planning a Lasting, Joyful Marriage* (Nashville: Thomas Nelson Publishers, n.d.), page 173.
5. Ed Wheat and Gloria Okes Perkins, *Love Life for Every Married Couple* (Grand Rapids: Zondervan Publishing House, Pyranee Books, 1980), page 80.
6. Walter Wangerin, Jr., *As for Me and My House: Crafting Your Marriage to Last* (Nashville: Thomas Nelson Publishers, 1987), page 191.
7. H. Norman Wright, *Understanding the Man in Your Life* (Waco, Tex.: Word Books, 1987), page 196.

"In the Integrity of My Heart"

I will walk within my house in the integrity of my heart.
Psalm 101:2

Integrity does not mean that I am perfect, but it does mean that I have an honest heart before God.[1]
Stephan Tchividjian

LESSON 11 Integrity in business, politics, and even the church is a challenging topic of discussion. Seldom, though, is anything said about integrity in the home. I feel quite strongly that if I cannot be the woman God wants me to be within the confines of my home, then I have no valid message or ministry outside my home. Integrity is honesty, uprightness, virtue, goodness, fairness: "the keeping of a commitment after the circumstances under which the commitment was made have changed or deteriorated."[2] Integrity is having a high sense of always wanting to do right and being willing to pay the price to do it.

Insight into Scripture

1. Herbert Lockyer wrote, "There is nothing in the entire range of biography sacred or profane, comparable to the idyllic simplicity, tenderness and beauty of the story of Ruth, the young widow of Moab."[3]

   Read the book of Ruth. Write a paragraph telling how you feel Ruth exemplifies integrity.

2. Matthew Henry made this observation of 1 Samuel 25:2-42: "We have here an account of Abigail's prudent management for the preserving of her husband and family from the destruction that was just coming upon them; and we find that she did her part admirably well and fully answered her character."[4]

   Read this passage and answer the following questions.

   a. How does Scripture describe Abigail?

b. How does Scripture describe Nabal?

c. Describe David's encounter with Abigail.

d. Why do you think Abigail waited to tell Nabal about what she had done?

e. Do you think that Abigail was justified in what she did? Why or why not?

f. Would you characterize Abigail as a woman of integrity? Why or why not?

---

3. The excellent, virtuous wife of Proverbs 31:10-31 seems to personify integrity. Read these verses carefully and list her relationships and qualities that exemplify her integrity.

> Trust allows him, encourages her, to be naked before you and not ashamed. Naked physically: no part of the body is hidden since no curve of it will be hurt or troubled by embarrassment. Naked emotionally and spiritually: no part of the personality, no feeling, no memory or fear or internal delight need be hidden either, since nothing of your spouse will be hurt or abused or embarrassed. Trust allows him, encourages her, to present a whole self before you. And honesty in you, likewise, hides nothing of your whole self from your spouse.[5]
>
> Walter Wangerin, Jr.

Insight into myself

4. a. Is my heart set on living righteously and honestly especially in my home? Why or why not?

b. How do I compromise my integrity in relating to my husband?

c. In what ways am I growing in my knowledge and understanding of Scripture and of God's leading so that I make right and fair responses in hard situations?

> Reader, how fares it with your family? Do you sing in the choir and sin in the chamber? Are you a saint abroad and a devil at home? For shame! What we are at home, that we are indeed.[6]
> Charles H. Spurgeon

Insight into my husband

5. a. Does my husband trust me in all areas of our life together? Why or why not?

b. Toward the end of my life, will my husband look back over our years together and praise me? Why or why not?

> Let me mention one more "cheap substitute" so common among Christian wives in our day. It is *learning about what's right rather than doing what is right.* . . . It has been my observation that a large percentage of Christian wives know more—much more—than they put into practice. And yet, they are continually interested in attending another class, taking another course, reading another book, going to another seminar . . . learning, discussing, studying, discovering. . . . And what results? Normally, greater guilt. Or, on the other side, an enormous backlog of theoretical data that blinds and thickens the conscience rather than spurs it into action. Learning more truth is a poor and cheap substitute for stopping and putting into action the truth already learned.[7]
> Charles R. Swindoll

Insight from an older woman

Ruth believed in the living God, the God of the Jews. She believed in Him so much that she was willing to travel to a foreign land with a bitter mother-in-law so that she could seek refuge under His wings. Even in hard circumstances she continued to serve Naomi and to trust God. Ruth kept her commitment, her vow to Naomi. She lived her integrity.

Abigail exemplifies integrity in an extremely difficult situation. Who of us would sit quietly and allow our husband to be murdered just because he had made a foolish decision? Abigail acted quickly and wisely for the good of her husband and home. The key to her decision is that it was truly for her husband's welfare; she literally did not have anything to gain for herself by what she did. She was courageous enough to do the right thing, "without being frightened by any fear" (1 Peter 3:6).

The wife in Proverbs 31 lived her life openly and honestly in her home. Interestingly, it is her family, mainly her husband, who praises her; it is not the poor, the needy, or the tradesmen. She lived uprightly because she feared God. She did not want to dishonor His name.

One major way this woman maintained her integrity was by living her priorities. As I have studied her life, I have observed that the first half of the verses list her priorities in order. The first comment about her is her excellence or virtue. This is a good indication that her relationship with God was first in her life. Her next priority is her husband. Verses 13-16 speak of her ministry to her children and her home. Verse 17 tells of her taking time for herself, and verses 19-20 describe her ministry to others outside the home.

Understanding our priorities helps us in making right decisions and commitments. Living our priorities is essential to becoming women who model integrity.

Part of fearing God is realizing that one day we will give an account of our lives—a major part of it as wives—to God. We will answer to Him for the materials we used to build our lives and marriages: whether gold, silver, or precious stones (basically living to do the will of God), or wood, hay, or stubble (basically living to please ourselves; see 1 Corinthians 3:10-15). To be women of integrity we must keep our commitments, have a keen sense of doing what is right before God, and live our priorities in honor and out of respect for our Lord. To live in this way, my friend, will enable us to stand unashamedly before our God and hear, "Well done, My good and faithful servant."

O LORD, who may abide in Thy tent?
Who may dwell on Thy holy hill?
He who walks with integrity, and works
righteousness,
And speaks truth in his heart.
Psalm 15:1-2

NOTES
1. Stephan Tchividjian, "The Evangelist's Inner Life," *Decision Magazine,* vol. 29, no. 5 (May 1988), page 12.
2. Unattributed quote from a taped speech by David Jeremiah, "Integrity," given at Forest Home retreat center in California, July 1986.
3. Herbert Lockyer, *All the Women of the Bible* (Grand Rapids: Zondervan Publishing House, 1967), page 149.
4. Matthew Henry, *Commentary on the Whole Bible,* vol. I (Iowa Falls, Iowa: Riverside Book & Bible House, n.d.), page 416.
5. Walter Wangerin, Jr., *As for Me and My House: Crafting Your Marriage to Last* (Nashville: Thomas Nelson Publishers, 1987), page 189.
6. Charles H. Spurgeon, *The Treasury of David,* vol. II, part 2 (McLean, Va.: MacDonald Publishing Co., n.d.), page 240.
7. Charles R. Swindoll, *Strike the Original Match* (Portland, Oreg.: Multnomah Press, 1980), page 59.

"I Press on Toward the Goal"

I press on toward the goal to win the prize for which God has called me heavenward in Christ Jesus.
Philippians 3:14 (NIV)

Our ultimate goal, our highest calling in life is to glorify God—not to be happy. Let that sink in! Glorifying Him is our greatest pursuit. Not to get our way. Not to be comfortable. Not to find fulfillment. Not even to be loved or to be appreciated or to be taken care of. Now these are important, but they are not primary.

As I glorify Him, He sees to it that other essential needs are met . . . or my need for them diminishes. Believe me, this concept will change your entire perspective on yourself, your life, and your marriage.[1]
Charles R. Swindoll

12

Often Jack will sign off his letters by writing "keep pressin'!" We do need to be encouraged to press on, to persevere, to keep our eyes on Jesus—to be reminded that our sole purpose is to bring glory to our gracious God. Certainly, life and marriage provide numerous opportunities for the need to keep going, to keep trusting, and to keep "pressin'."

Insight into Scripture

1. a. Scripture is rich in passages that exhort us to perseverance in our purpose to glorify the Lord. Read the following passages and write down how they encourage your faithfulness.

   1 Corinthians 10:31

   2 Corinthians 4:7-11

   2 Corinthians 4:16-18

   Philippians 3:7-14

   Colossians 3:23-24

   Hebrews 12:1-3

b. Which of these scriptures help you the most in continuing to honor God and be a godly wife? Why?

The truth about marriage is that it is a way not of avoiding any of the painful trials and subtractions of life, but rather of confronting them, of exposing and tackling them most intimately, most humanly. It is a way to meet suffering personally, head on, with the peculiar directness, the reckless candidness characteristic only of love. It is a way of living life with no other strategy or defense or protection than that of love. . . . Marriage is a way not to evade suffering, but to suffer purposefully.[2]
Mike Mason

Insight into myself

2. a. As a woman who loves God, what is my purpose?

b. As a wife who loves God, what is my purpose?

c. What are my greatest struggles in fulfilling this purpose in my marriage?

d. What are my greatest joys in fulfilling this purpose in my marriage?

e. As I end this study, what is my earnest prayer?

A proper understanding of marriage as a calling to high ministry will cause us to look at the deepest needs of our mates and to appreciate our unique opportunity to touch those needs in significant ways. . . . Christians who have put God to the test by vulnerably surrendering to His will, examining their motives regularly to see where they are protecting themselves rather than ministering, are tasting the goodness of God. These people more and more see their marriage commitment as an opportunity to pursue their deepest desires, to follow a good path and to invite their spouses to walk with them.[3]
Lawrence J. Crabb, Jr.

Insight into my husband

3. a. If there were one thing my husband would want me to do, or stop doing, to honor or please him in a godly way, what would that be? Am I willing to do it (why or why not)?

b. What is my prayer for my husband?

Gifting your spouse, volunteering *whether he deserves it or not,* for no reason whatsoever, for no payment in exchange, gratuitously, perfectly freely, for his sake alone, regardless of his work, his worth, or his investment in the relationship; giving him something for nothing—this is *Grace.* This displaces the marriage contract again and again with newness. And this images in action the divine face of the Lord Jesus Christ. As Jesus loved, so do you show the same love to your spouse.[4]

Walter Wangerin, Jr.

Insight from an older woman

Someone has defined glorify as "giving the correct estimate of." I like this idea because if I desire to glorify the Lord, then my life will consistently give others the right opinion or thought of who God is and how He undergirds my life and makes a difference in the way I live. I think that this is the essence of Peter's writing concerning wives not saying a word to a husband who is not obedient to the Word. A wife who truly trusts God, who looks to Him for love and strength, and who wants, above all, to represent her Lord faithfully, will be content to let her life speak to her husband.

This life that the Lord calls us to is *real.* His grace *is* sufficient, He ways *are* just, His love *is* complete, and His care *is* personal. He wants us to fix our hope on Him and on things that are eternal. We are out of Eden, but our stay is only temporary. Our permanent home is prepared for us in Heaven.

I love God so much. More than anything I desire to please Him. I so want to finish the race, to keep an eternal perspective, to do all that I do for His glory, and to really know Him and the power of His resurrection and the fellowship of His sufferings. This is my purpose and this is my prayer, and so I press on toward the goal to win the prize for which God has called me heavenward in Christ Jesus.

It will be worth it all when we see Jesus,
Life's trials will seem so small when we see Christ;
One glimpse of His dear face all sorrow will erase,
So bravely run the race 'til we see Christ.[5]
Esther Kerr Rusthoi

NOTES
1. Charles R. Swindoll, *Strike the Original Match* (Portland, Oreg.: Multnomah Press, 1980), page 165.
2. Mike Mason, *The Mystery of Marriage* (Portland, Oreg.: Multnomah Press, 1985), page 142.
3. Lawrence J. Crabb, Jr., *The Marriage Builder* (Grand Rapids: Zondervan Publishing House, 1982), page 119.
4. Walter Wangerin, Jr., *As for Me and My House: Crafting Your Marriage to Last* (Nashville: Thomas Nelson Publishers, 1987), page 251.
5. From the hymn "When We See Christ," by Esther Kerr Rusthoi, in *Hymns for the Family of God* (Nashville: Paragon Associates, Inc., 1976), pages 129-130.

SMALL-GROUP MATERIALS FROM NAVPRESS

BIBLE STUDY SERIES

DESIGN FOR DISCIPLESHIP
GOD IN YOU
GOD'S DESIGN FOR THE FAMILY
INSTITUTE OF BIBLICAL
   COUNSELING Series

LIFECHANGE
LOVE ONE ANOTHER
RADICAL RELATIONSHIPS
SPIRITUAL DISCIPLINES
STUDIES IN CHRISTIAN LIVING
THINKING THROUGH DISCIPLESHIP

TOPICAL BIBLE STUDIES

Becoming a Woman of Excellence
Becoming a Woman of Freedom
Becoming a Woman of Prayer
Becoming a Woman of Purpose
The Blessing Study Guide
Homemaking
Intimacy with God
Loving Your Husband

Loving Your Wife
A Mother's Legacy
Praying From God's Heart
Surviving Life in the Fast Lane
To Run and Not Grow Tired
To Walk and Not Grow Weary
What God Does When Men Pray
When the Squeeze Is On

BIBLE STUDIES WITH COMPANION BOOKS

Bold Love
Daughters of Eve
The Discipline of Grace
The Feminine Journey
Inside Out
The Masculine Journey
The Practice of Godliness
The Pursuit of Holiness

Secret Longings of the Heart
Spiritual Disciplines
Tame Your Fears
Transforming Grace
Trusting God
What Makes a Man?
The Wounded Heart

RESOURCES

Brothers!
Discipleship Journal's Best
   Small-Group Ideas
How to Build a Small Groups Ministry
How to Lead Small Groups
Jesus Cares for Women
The Navigator Bible Studies
   Handbook

The Small Group Leaders
   Training Course
Topical Memory System
   (KJV/NIV and NASB/NKJV)
Topical Memory System:
   Life Issues